Patriotology Trivia Challenge

New England Patriots Football

Patriotology Trivia Challenge

New England Patriots Football

Researched by Paul F. Wilson

Paul F. Wilson & Tom P. Rippey III, Editors

Kick The Ball, Ltd
Lewis Center, Ohio

Trivia by Kick The Ball, Ltd

College Football Trivia

Alabama Crimson Tide	Auburn Tigers	Boston College Eagles	Florida Gators
Georgia Bulldogs	LSU Tigers	Miami Hurricanes	Michigan Wolverines
Nebraska Cornhuskers	Notre Dame Fighting Irish	Ohio State Buckeyes	Oklahoma Sooners
Oregon Ducks	Penn State Nittany Lions	Southern Cal Trojans	Texas Longhorns

Pro Football Trivia

Arizona Cardinals	Baltimore Ravens	Buffalo Bills	Chicago Bears
Cleveland Browns	Dallas Cowboys	Denver Broncos	Green Bay Packers
Indianapolis Colts	Kansas City Chiefs	Minnesota Vikings	New England Patriots
New Orleans Saints	New York Giants	New York Jets	Oakland Raiders
Philadelphia Eagles	Pittsburgh Steelers	San Francisco 49ers	Washington Redskins

Pro Baseball Trivia

Atlanta Braves	Baltimore Orioles	Boston Red Sox	Chicago Cubs
Chicago White Sox	Cincinnati Reds	Detroit Tigers	Houston Astros
Los Angeles Dodgers	Milwaukee Brewers	Minnesota Twins	New York Mets
New York Yankees	Philadelphia Phillies	Saint Louis Cardinals	San Francisco Giants

College Basketball Trivia

Duke Blue Devils	Georgetown Hoyas	Indiana Hoosiers	Kansas Jayhawks
Kentucky Wildcats	Maryland Terrapins	Michigan State Spartans	North Carolina Tar Heels
Syracuse Orange	UConn Huskies	UCLA Bruins	

Pro Basketball Trivia

Boston Celtics	Chicago Bulls	Detroit Pistons	Los Angeles Lakers
Utah Jazz			

Visit **www.TriviaGameBooks.com** for more details.

In my life's travels I have come to know each of the following individuals who proudly call themselves New England Patriots fans:

*Linda O'Donnell, Dan Bukkhegyi,
Eric Hokanson, John Henderson, Maisie Mulcahy,
Eric Asendorf, Jan Chadie and Matt Hart*

This book is dedicated to them.

Patriotology Trivia Challenge: New England Patriots Football; Second Edition 2011

Published by
Kick The Ball, Ltd
8595 Columbus Pike, Suite 197
Lewis Center, OH 43035
www.TriviaGameBooks.com

Edited by: Paul F. Wilson & Tom P. Rippey III
Copy Edited by: Ashley Thomas Memory
Designed and Formatted by: Paul F. Wilson
Researched by: Paul F. Wilson

Copyright © 2011 by Kick The Ball, Ltd, Lewis Center, Ohio

ALL RIGHTS RESERVED. No part of this book may be reproduced or transmitted in any form whatsoever, electronic, or mechanical, including photocopying, recording, or by any informational storage or retrieval system without the expressed written, dated and signed permission from the copyright holder.

Trademarks and Copyrights: Kick The Ball, Ltd is not associated with any event, team, conference, or league mentioned in this book. All trademarks are the property of their respective owners. Kick The Ball, Ltd respects and honors the copyrights and trademarks of others. We use event, team, conference, or league names only as points of reference in titles, questions, answers, and other sections of our trivia game books. Names, statistics, and others facts obtained through public domain resources.

LIMIT OF LIABILITY/DISCLAIMER OF WARRANTY: THE RESEARCHER AND PUBLISHER HAVE USED GREAT CARE IN RESEARCHING AND WRITING THIS BOOK. HOWEVER, WE MAKE NO REPRESENTATION OR WARRANTIES AS TO THE COMPLETENESS OF ITS CONTENTS OR THEIR ACCURACY AND WE SPECIFICALLY DISCLAIM ANY IMPLIED WARRANTIES OF MERCHANTABILITY OR FITNESS FOR A PARTICULAR PURPOSE. WARRANTIES MAY NOT BE CREATED OR EXTENDED BY ANY SALES MATERIALS OR SALESPERSON OF THIS BOOK. NEITHER THE RESEARCHER NOR THE PUBLISHER SHALL BE LIABLE FOR ANY LOSS OF PROFIT OR ANY OTHER COMMERCIAL DAMAGES, INCLUDING BUT NOT LIMITED TO SPECIAL, INCIDENTAL, CONSEQUENTIAL, OR OTHER DAMAGES.

For information on ordering this book in bulk at reduced prices, please email us at pfwilson@triviagamebooks.com.

International Standard Book Number: 978-1-613320-009-4
Printed and Bound in the United States of America
10 9 8 7 6 5 4 3 2 1

Table of Contents

How to Play……………………………………………………….. Page 1

First Quarter – 1-Point Questions (Questions 1-50)………………. Page 3

First Quarter Patriot Cool Fact…………...………………………. Page 16

First Quarter Answer Key……………………………...………... Page 17

Second Quarter – 2-Point Questions (Questions 1-50)…………... Page 23

Second Quarter Patriot Cool Fact……….……………………….. Page 36

Second Quarter Answer Key……………………………………... Page 37

Third Quarter – 3-Point Questions (Questions 1-50)……………... Page 42

Third Quarter Patriot Cool Fact……….………………………….. Page 55

Third Quarter Answer Key……………………………………….. Page 56

Fourth Quarter – 4-Point Questions (Questions 1-50)……………. Page 61

Fourth Quarter Patriot Cool Fact……….………………………… Page 74

Fourth Quarter Answer Key……………………………………… Page 75

Overtime Bonus – 4-Point Questions (Questions 1-10)…….......… Page 80

Overtime Bonus Answer Key…………………...……………….. Page 83

Player / Team Score Sheet……………….……………………….. Page 85

Dear Friend,

Thank you for purchasing our ***Patriotology Trivia Challenge*** game book!

We have made every attempt to verify the accuracy of the questions and answers contained in this book. However it is still possible that from time to time an error has been made by us or our researchers. In the event you find a question or answer that is questionable or inaccurate, we ask for your understanding and thank you for bringing it to our attention so we may improve future editions of this book. Please email us at tprippey@triviagamebooks.com with those observations and comments.

Have fun playing ***Patriotology Trivia Challenge***!

Paul & Tom

Paul Wilson and Tom Rippey
Co-Founders, Kick The Ball, Ltd

PS – You can discover more about all of our current trivia game books by visiting www.TriviaGameBooks.com.

How to Play
Patriotology Trivia Challenge

Book Format:

There are four quarters, each made up of fifty questions. Each quarter's questions have assigned point values. Questions are designed to get progressively more difficult as you proceed through each quarter, as well as through the book itself. Most questions are in a four-option multiple-choice format so that you will at least have a 25% chance of getting a correct answer for some of the more challenging questions.

We have even added Overtime in the event of a tie, or just in case you want to keep playing a little longer.

Game Options:

One Player -
To play on your own, simply answer each of the questions in all the quarters, and in the overtime section, if you'd like. Use the Player / Team Score Sheet to record your answers and the quarter Answer Keys to check your answers. Calculate each quarter's points and the total for the game at the bottom of the Player / Team Score Sheet to determine your final score.

Two or More Players –
To play with multiple players decide if you will all be competing with each other individually, or if you will form and play as teams. Each player / team will then have its own Player / Team Score Sheet to record its answer. You can use the quarter Answer Keys to check your answers and to calculate your final scores.

How to Play
Patriotology Trivia Challenge

The Player / Team Score Sheets have been designed so that each team can answer all questions or you can divide the questions up in any combination you would prefer. For example, you may want to alternate questions if two players are playing or answer every third question for three players, etc. In any case, simply record your response to your questions in the corresponding quarter and question number on the Player / Team Score Sheet.

A winner will be determined by multiplying the total number of correct answers for each quarter by the point value per quarter, then adding together the final total for all quarters combined. Play the game again and again by alternating the questions that your team is assigned so that you will answer a different set of questions each time you play.

You Create the Game -
There are countless other ways of using **Patriotology Trivia Challenge** questions. It is limited only to your imagination. Examples might be using them at your tailgate or other professional football related party. Players / Teams who answer questions incorrectly may have to perform a required action, or winners may receive special prizes. Let us know what other games you come up with!

Have fun!

First Quarter — 1-Point Questions
Patriotology Trivia Challenge

1) What was the name of the original owner of the Boston Patriots?

   A) Victor Kiam
   B) Billy Sullivan Jr.
   C) James Orthwein
   D) Robert Kraft

Answers begin on page 17

2) What are the Patriots' team colors?

   A) Midnight Blue, Bright Red and White or Silver
   B) Blue, Red and Sterling Silver
   C) Navy Blue, Bright Red, Silver & Sharp White
   D) Nautical Blue, Red, New Century Silver & White

3) New England's stadium has an official seating capacity greater than 70,000.

   A) True
   B) False

4) What year did the Pats play their first-ever game?

   A) 1955
   B) 1959
   C) 1960
   D) 1963

New England Patriots Football

First Quarter — 1-Point Questions
Patriotology Trivia Challenge

5) What was Patriots head coach Lou Saban's nickname?

   A) Saber
   B) Trader Lou
   C) Lou-Lou
   D) Tiger

6) In which NFL division does New England play?

   A) AFC East
   B) AFC North
   C) AFC South
   D) AFC West

7) What is the name of the song played when the Patriots take the field?

   A) "Song 2"
   B) "Carmina Burana"
   C) "Elevation"
   D) "All Hail to Massachusetts"

8) How many times did the Patriots play the College All-Stars?

   A) 1
   B) 2
   C) 3
   D) None of the above

New England Patriots Football

First Quarter — 1-Point Questions
Patriotology Trivia Challenge

9) Did the Patriots play in the NFL in a season in which the "Bonus Choice" No. 1 draft pick was used?

   A) Yes
   B) No

10) Who was the first-ever player to be signed by the Patriots?

   A) Gino Cappelletti
   B) Bob Lee
   C) Harvey White
   D) Dick Christy

11) Who was the most recent Patriot head coach to win NFL Coach of the Year?

   A) Bill Parcells
   B) Chuck Fairbanks
   C) Raymond Berry
   D) Bill Belichick

12) The Ravens have never beaten New England in Foxborough.

   A) True
   B) False

First Quarter — 1-Point Questions
Patriotology Trivia Challenge

13) What is the nickname of Gillette Stadium?

   A) The Borough
   B) The Fox
   C) The Gill
   D) The Razor

14) To what classical piece does the End Zone Militia fire their flintlock muskets following a point after touchdown (PAT) by the Pats?

   A) Handel's "Messiah"
   B) Beethoven's "Symphony No. 9"
   C) Tchaikovsky's "1812 Overture"
   D) Mozart's "Requiem"

15) What year did Gillette Stadium open?

   A) 1996
   B) 1998
   C) 2000
   D) 2002

16) How many times have the Pats played in a Monday Night Football game?

   A) 42
   B) 47
   C) 53
   D) 58

New England Patriots Football

First Quarter — 1-Point Questions
Patriotology Trivia Challenge

17) What position did Bill Belichick play in college?

    A) Guard and Tackle
    B) Center and Tight End
    C) Nose Guard and Defensive End
    D) He did not play college football

18) From which university has New England drafted the most players?

    A) Notre Dame
    B) Ohio State
    C) Michigan
    D) Boston College

19) Who holds New England's career rushing record?

    A) Jim Nance
    B) Sam Cunningham
    C) Tony Collins
    D) Curtis Martin

20) How many Patriots were named NFL Rookie of the Week in 2010?

    A) 0
    B) 1
    C) 2
    D) 3

New England Patriots Football

First Quarter — 1-Point Questions
Patriotology Trivia Challenge

21) Did Tom Brady win his first game as a starter for the Patriots?

    A) Yes
    B) No

22) Where do the Patriots hold their training camp?

    A) Brockton, Mass.
    B) Boston, Mass.
    C) Foxborough, Mass.
    D) Mansfield, Mass.

23) Which New England head coach has the most overall regular-season wins?

    A) Mike Holovak
    B) Chuck Fairbanks
    C) Raymond Berry
    D) Bill Belichick

24) How many owners has New England had in its team history?

    A) 2
    B) 4
    C) 5
    D) 7

First Quarter — 1-Point Questions
Patriotology Trivia Challenge

25) Who holds New England's record for passing yards in a single game?

   A) Drew Bledsoe
   B) Tom Brady
   C) Steve Grogan
   D) Jim Plunkett

26) Which one of the following is not a name by which New England's home field was known from 1971-2001?

   A) Schaefer Stadium
   B) Sullivan Stadium
   C) Foxboro Stadium
   D) Kraft Stadium

27) How many times has New England played in the Super Bowl?

   A) 4
   B) 6
   C) 7
   D) 9

28) What year did the Patriots silhouette helmet logo, nicknamed the "Flying Elvis" by fans, first appear?

   A) 1981
   B) 1991
   C) 1993
   D) 2000

New England Patriots Football

First Quarter — 1-Point Questions
Patriotology Trivia Challenge

29) Have the Patriots ever played the Colts in the playoffs?

   A) Yes
   B) No

30) Who is the only player to gain greater than 2,000 total yards for the Patriots in one season?

   A) Corey Dillon
   B) Curtis Martin
   C) Jim Nance
   D) None of the above

31) Who led the Patriots in sacks during the 2010 regular season?

   A) Rob Ninkovich
   B) Mike Wright
   C) Gerard Warren
   D) Tully Banta-Cain

32) Which of these teams has New England played the most in postseason games?

   A) Indianapolis Colts
   B) Oakland Raiders
   C) Miami Dolphins
   D) Jacksonville Jaguars

First Quarter — 1-Point Questions
Patriotology Trivia Challenge

33) What are the most regular-season wins the Patriots have had in a single season?

    A) 14
    B) 15
    C) 16
    D) None of the above

34) Which Patriot holds the NFL record for the most passes attempted in a game?

    A) Drew Bledsoe
    B) Tom Brady
    C) Tony Eason
    D) Steve Grogan

35) How many defensive touchdowns did the Patriots have in 2010?

    A) 0
    B) 2
    C) 4
    D) 6

36) What single-season NFL record did the Patriots set in 1978?

    A) Fewest First Downs, Rushing
    B) Fewest First Downs, Penalty
    C) Most First Downs, Penalty
    D) Most First Downs, Rushing

New England Patriots Football

First Quarter — 1-Point Questions
Patriotology Trivia Challenge

37) Who is the Patriots' play-by-play radio announcer?

   A) Gil Santos
   B) Gino Cappelletti
   C) Dale Arnold
   D) Jon Morris

38) A player from which team injured Patriots quarterback Tom Brady's left knee in the 2008 season opener?

   A) Kansas City Chiefs
   B) San Diego Chargers
   C) Oakland Raiders
   D) Denver Broncos

39) In which year was the Patriots 35th Anniversary Team selected by members of the local New England media?

   A) 1993
   B) 1994
   C) 1995
   D) 1996

40) Who was New England's last opponent of the 2010 regular season?

   A) Pittsburgh Steelers
   B) New York Jets
   C) Miami Dolphins
   D) New York Giants

First Quarter — 1-Point Questions
Patriotology Trivia Challenge

41) Including the playoffs, against which team does New England have the lowest all-time winning percentage?

   A) Dallas Cowboys
   B) San Francisco 49ers
   C) Washington Redskins
   D) Carolina Panthers

42) Who holds New England's record for the most pass receptions in a rookie season?

   A) Terry Glenn
   B) Irving Fryar
   C) Stanley Morgan
   D) Gino Cappelletti

43) Who was New England's opponent in the controversial "Snow Bowl" game of 2002?

   A) Indianapolis Colts
   B) Pittsburgh Steelers
   C) Jacksonville Jaguars
   D) Oakland Raiders

44) How many NFL Championships has New England won?

   A) 2
   B) 3
   C) 4
   D) 5

New England Patriots Football

First Quarter — 1-Point Questions
Patriotology Trivia Challenge

45) Which Patriot holds the team's single-game rushing record (yards)?

   A) Corey Dillon
   B) Curtis Martin
   C) Tony Collins
   D) Sam Cunningham

46) Who was the most recent Patriot to win the Super Bowl MVP Award?

   A) Tom Brady
   B) Laurence Maroney
   C) Adam Vinatieri
   D) Deion Branch

47) How many one-season (or less) head coaches has New England had?

   A) 1
   B) 3
   C) 5
   D) 6

48) Did Mike Holovak coach another NFL team after leaving the Patriots?

   A) Yes
   B) No

First Quarter — 1-Point Questions
Patriotology Trivia Challenge

49) Who holds the New England record for points scored in a career?

   A) Gino Cappelletti
   B) Tony Franklin
   C) John Smith
   D) Adam Vinatieri

50) In which year did the Patriots first celebrate a victory over the Colts?

   A) 1970
   B) 1971
   C) 1973
   D) 1975

First Quarter — Cool Fact
Patriotology Trivia Challenge

Among the many team and NFL records set since Coach Bill Belichick joined the New England Patriots in 2000 is one of particular significance. As NFL fans who closely follow the game's history can attest, some of the greatest teams in history were coached by Hall of Fame coaches such as Chuck Noll, Joe Gibbs, Bill Walsh and Tom Landry. Their teams set myriad playoff and Super Bowl records as they cemented their legendary statuses. Yet one thing none of them can claim is winning three Super Bowl Championships in four consecutive NFL seasons. This unique and enviable accomplishment belongs only to Coach Belichick of the New England Patriots. From 2001-04, under the watchful eye of Coach Belichick, New England exerted dominance over the league like no other team in the Super Bowl era. During those seasons, Coach Belichick led the Pats to victories in Super Bowls XXXVI, XXXVIII and XXXIX.

First Quarter — Answer Key
Patriotology Trivia Challenge

1) B – Billy Sullivan Jr. (Sullivan was a prolific sportswriter and businessman who paid $25,000 for the rights to the eighth and final team in the inaugural season of the American Football League.)

2) D – Nautical Blue, Red, New Century Silver & White (All of these colors are noted as being official team colors.)

3) B – False (Official stadium capacity is listed as 68,756 for football.)

4) C – 1960 (The Patriots' first-ever official game was also the first-ever official preseason game of the fledgling AFL played on July 30, 1960.)

5) B – Trader Lou (It is said that Lou Saban was admired by his players, who affectionately referred to him by this nickname.)

6) A – AFC East (Other AFC East members include Buffalo, NY Jets and Miami.)

7) B – "Carmina Burana" (Composed by Carl Orff circa 1935-36. "Crazy Train" by Ozzy Osborne can also be heard following "Carmina Burana.")

8) D – None of the above (The Patriots never won an NFL Championship during the years [1934-1976] that this annual preseason game was played.)

9) B – No (The Bonus Choice methodology was used for only 12 seasons from 1947-58.)

First Quarter — Answer Key
Patriotology Trivia Challenge

10) C – Harvey White (White, a quarterback from Clemson, signed his contract with the Boston Patriots on Dec. 20, 1959.)

11) D – Bill Belichick (Belichick was named AP & Maxwell Football Club NFL Coach of the Year in 2007.)

12) A – False (On Jan. 10, 2010, the Ravens took their first-ever victory from the Patriots in Foxborough [New England 14, Baltimore 33].)

13) D – The Razor (The nickname is given to the stadium by local fans and the media.)

14) C – Tchaikovsky's "1812 Overture" (The EZM fire a salute following each Patriot score and a volley at the end of a victorious game.)

15) D – 2002 (Groundbreaking for the stadium was in 2000, with the grand opening on Sept. 9, 2002.)

16) A – 42 (The Pats have an all-time record of 20-22 [.476] in Monday Night Football games.)

17) B – Center and Tight End (Belichick played both center and tight end for Wesleyan University.)

18) D – Boston College (All time, New England has drafted 19 players from BC. The most recent player was DT Ron Brace in 2009.)

19) B – Sam Cunningham (From 1973-79 and 1981-82 Cunningham had 5,453 yards on 1,385 attempts in 107 games.)

First Quarter — Answer Key
Patriotology Trivia Challenge

20) D – 3 (Rob Gronkowski received the honor twice [Weeks 14 and 17] and Aaron Hernandez once [Week 15].)
21) A – Yes (Brady started his first-ever game after Drew Bledsoe's injury in Week 2 of the 2001 season. He led the Pats to a 44-13 win over the rival Colts.)
22) C – Foxborough, Mass. (Training camps are held at Gillette Stadium and its practice fields.)
23) D – Bill Belichick (Coach Belichick has 126 career victories as the Pats' head coach.)
24) B – 4 (Bill Sullivan Jr. from 1959-88, Victor Kiam from 1988-92, James B. Orthwein from 1992-94 and Robert K. Kraft from 1994-present)
25) A – Drew Bledsoe (On Nov. 13, 1994, Bledsoe passed for 426 yards vs. Minnesota in a 26-20 overtime victory.)
26) D – Kraft Stadium (Foxboro Stadium was also called Schaefer Stadium from 1971-83 and Sullivan Stadium from 1983-89.)
27) B – 6 (The Pats appeared in Super Bowls: XX, XXXI, XXXVI, XXXVIII, XXXIX and XLII.)
28) C – 1993 (The logo was changed during James Orthwein's short ownership of the team.)
29) A – Yes (The Colts beat the Patriots, 38-34, in the 2006-07 AFC Championship Game held on Jan. 21, 2007. However, the Pats beat the Colts in the 2004-05 [24-14] and 2005-06 [20-3] NFL playoffs.)

New England Patriots Football

First Quarter — Answer Key
Patriotology Trivia Challenge

30) D – None of the above (Corey Dillon holds the Pats' single-season record with 1,738 total yards [1,635 rushing and 103 receiving] in 2004.)

31) B – Mike Wright (Wright led all Patriots defenders with 5.5 sacks in 2010.)

32) D – Jacksonville Jaguars (New England has faced Jacksonville four times in the playoffs [3-1]. They have also played Pittsburgh four times resulting in the same 3-1 record.)

33) C – 16 (The Pats finished the 2007 regular season with a perfect 16-0 record.)

34) A – Drew Bledsoe (Bledsoe had 70 pass attempts versus Minnesota on Nov. 13, 1994.)

35) D – 6 (Patriot defenders accounted for six defensive touchdowns in the 2010 regular season.)

36) D – Most First Downs, Rushing (The Pats rushed for 181 first downs that season. Los Angeles is second all time in that category with 177.)

37) A – Gil Santos (Santos has been the Patriots play-by-play announcer since 1995. Gino Cappelletti joins him in the booth as the broadcast's color commentator.)

38) A – Kansas City Chiefs (Safety Bernard Pollard's hit took Brady out of the game midway through the game's first quarter.)

39) B – 1994 (The team includes three special teams players, 12 defensive players and 11 offensive players.)

New England Patriots Football

First Quarter — Answer Key
Patriotology Trivia Challenge

40) C – Miami Dolphins (New England easily took care of the Dolphins in their season finale, in a final score of 38-7.)

41) C – Washington Redskins (New England's all-time record versus Washington is 2-6 [.250].)

42) A – Terry Glenn (Glenn's 90 receptions in 1996 also rank him second of all time in the NFL.)

43) D – Oakland Raiders (Played in Foxborough, Adam Vinatieri's two consecutive field goals late in the game [one in regulation and one in overtime] sealed the win for the Pats.)

44) B – 3 (New England's league championships have all occurred in the new millennium: 2001, 2003 and 2004.)

45) C – Tony Collins (Collins carried the ball for 212 yards on 23 attempts versus the NY Jets on Sept. 18, 1983.)

46) D – Deion Branch (Patriots wide receiver Deion Branch won Super Bowl XXXIX MVP.)

47) B – 3 (Phil Bengtson [interim head coach 1972 season], Hank Bullough, co-head coach 1978 season and Rod Rust [head coach 1990])

48) A – Yes (Coach Holovak left the Patriots following the 1968 season. In 1976 he led the NY Jets in a single game as head coach.)

First Quarter — Answer Key
Patriotology Trivia Challenge

49) D – Adam Vinatieri (Vinatieri had 1,158 career points from 1996-2005.)

50) B – 1971 (After three straight losses to the Colts, the Pats defeated them 21-17 on Dec. 19, 1971.)

Note: All answers valid as of the end of the 2010 season, unless otherwise indicated in the question itself.

Second Quarter — 2-Point Questions
Patriotology Trivia Challenge

1) What is the name of the regional entertainment and retail center located on Gillette Stadium's grounds?

   A) Patriot Place
   B) Hall of Patriots
   C) Patriots Hall Place
   D) Patriots Town Center

Answers begin on page 37

2) What jersey number did Patriots quarterback Steve Grogan wear?

   A) No. 7
   B) No. 10
   C) No. 12
   D) No. 14

3) When was the last time the Patriots drafted a running back in the first round of the NFL Draft?

   A) 2006
   B) 2007
   C) 2008
   D) 2011

4) In which decade did New England have the highest winning percentage?

   A) 1970s
   B) 1980s
   C) 1990s
   D) 2000s

New England Patriots Football

Second Quarter — 2-Point Questions
Patriotology Trivia Challenge

5) Does New England have an all-time winning record against Indianapolis?

    A) Yes
    B) No

6) What is New England's all-time record for the most consecutive regular seasons with 10 wins or more?

    A) 6
    B) 8
    C) 10
    D) 12

7) What were the most rushing yards by the Patriots in a Super Bowl?

    A) 43
    B) 92
    C) 112
    D) 156

8) Where did former Patriots head coach Pete Carroll play college football?

    A) Pacific
    B) Notre Dame
    C) Miami of Ohio
    D) Oregon

Second Quarter — 2-Point Questions
Patriotology Trivia Challenge

9) For which university did the Patriots Ty Law and Tom Brady play?

   A) Miami
   B) Missouri
   C) Michigan State
   D) Michigan

10) How many teams has New England played 50 or more times in the regular and postseasons combined?

   A) 4
   B) 5
   C) 7
   D) 8

11) What are the most points the Patriots have allowed in a playoff game?

   A) 36
   B) 42
   C) 51
   D) 63

12) Against which team was New England's first-ever league win?

   A) Denver Broncos
   B) Buffalo Bills
   C) Dallas Texans
   D) Oakland Raiders

Second Quarter — 2-Point Questions
Patriotology Trivia Challenge

13) Does Brian Hoyer have greater than 50 career passing attempts?

   A) Yes
   B) No

14) When was the last time a player gained over 200 yards rushing in a game against New England?

   A) 1969
   B) 1974
   C) 1995
   D) 2002

15) What is the record for the longest field goal kicked by a Patriot at home?

   A) 50 yards
   B) 51 yards
   C) 54 yards
   D) 59 yards

16) How many yards was Ellis Hobbs' NFL record-setting kickoff return versus the New York Jets in 2007?

   A) 108
   B) 109
   C) 110
   D) None of the above

New England Patriots Football

Second Quarter — 2-Point Questions
Patriotology Trivia Challenge

17) In how many games in 2007 did Pats quarterback Tom Brady have three or more touchdown passes?

   A) 7
   B) 9
   C) 10
   D) 12

18) When was the last time the Patriots had over 500 yards of total offense in a game?

   A) 1996
   B) 2002
   C) 2007
   D) 2010

19) How many times has New England had the No. 1 overall draft pick in the NFL Draft?

   A) 2
   B) 4
   C) 5
   D) 7

20) His job at New England is Bill Belichick's second head coaching position.

   A) True
   B) False

Second Quarter — 2-Point Questions
Patriotology Trivia Challenge

21) How many yards is the longest rushing play in New England history?

    A) 75
    B) 77
    C) 80
    D) 85

22) Since the Carolina Panthers joined the league in 1995, how many times have the Pats played them?

    A) 5
    B) 9
    C) 13
    D) 17

23) In which year was Gillette Stadium's surface changed from grass to FieldTurf?

    A) 2004
    B) 2006
    C) 2008
    D) None of the above

24) How many times has New England played in the AFC Wild Card Playoff Game?

    A) 2
    B) 3
    C) 5
    D) 7

Second Quarter — 2-Point Questions
Patriotology Trivia Challenge

25) The Patriots have never been outgained in a Super Bowl appearance.

   A) True
   B) False

26) In which year did the Patriots win their first-ever playoff game?

   A) 1960
   B) 1961
   C) 1962
   D) 1963

27) How many times has New England lost a home opener (first game played in Mass.)?

   A) 6
   B) 9
   C) 12
   D) 15

28) Which of these Patriots was not named NFL Offensive Rookie of the Year?

   A) John Smith
   B) Curtis Martin
   C) John Stephens
   D) Leonard Russell

New England Patriots Football

Second Quarter — 2-Point Questions
Patriotology Trivia Challenge

29) How many years did Steve Grogan play football for the Patriots?

- A) 12
- B) 13
- C) 15
- D) 16

30) How many games did New England play in its first NFL season?

- A) 13
- B) 14
- C) 15
- D) 16

31) What is New England's record for the longest punt?

- A) 82 yards
- B) 87 yards
- C) 89 yards
- D) 93 yards

32) Coach Belichick is only one of three NFL head coaches to ever lead his team to an undefeated regular season.

- A) True
- B) False

Second Quarter — 2-Point Questions
Patriotology Trivia Challenge

33) Who was the most recent Patriot to have greater than 100 receptions in a single season?

   A) Troy Brown
   B) Randy Moss
   C) Wes Welker
   D) Deion Branch

34) Who is the only Patriot receiver to gain over 200 yards in a single game?

   A) Irving Fryar
   B) Harold Jackson
   C) Stanley Morgan
   D) Terry Glenn

35) To which team did New England suffer its worst loss during its first-ever season?

   A) Houston Oilers
   B) Dallas Texans
   C) Buffalo Bills
   D) L.A. Chargers

36) Who was New England's first-ever opponent at Gillette Stadium?

   A) Pittsburgh Steelers
   B) New York Jets
   C) Kansas City Chiefs
   D) San Diego Chargers

Second Quarter — 2-Point Questions
Patriotology Trivia Challenge

37) When was the last time the Pats scored a touchdown on their first offense drive of the season?

   A) 1987
   B) 1997
   C) 2007
   D) 2010

38) Which of these Patriots has played in the most Pro Bowls?

   A) John Hannah
   B) Drew Bledsoe
   C) Bruce Armstrong
   D) Jon Morris

39) Who holds New England's record for passing yards in a single season?

   A) Tony Eason
   B) Tom Brady
   C) Drew Bledsoe
   D) Steve Grogan

40) In 2007, Pats kicker Stephen Gostkowski set the NFL record for the most PATs in a season.

   A) True
   B) False

Second Quarter — 2-Point Questions
Patriotology Trivia Challenge

41) Who holds New England's record for the longest reception for a touchdown?

   A) Craig James
   B) David Patten
   C) Randy Vataha
   D) Terry Glenn

42) Excluding 2008, when was the last season Tom Brady did not start all 16 regular-season games for New England?

   A) 1999
   B) 2000
   C) 2001
   D) 2003

43) When was the last time the Patriots had a punt blocked?

   A) 2003
   B) 2005
   C) 2006
   D) 2009

44) Patriot Steve Nelson recovered three opponent fumbles in a game against which team in 1978?

   A) Chicago Bears
   B) Philadelphia Eagles
   C) Denver Broncos
   D) San Francisco 49ers

New England Patriots Football

Second Quarter — 2-Point Questions
Patriotology Trivia Challenge

45) Did Drew Bledsoe have greater than 30,000 career passing yards at New England?

   A) Yes
   B) No

46) Who holds the Patriots' record for career sacks?

   A) Julius Adams
   B) Willie McGinest
   C) Mike Vrabel
   D) Andre Tippett

47) How many Patriots have greater than 1,250 yards receiving in a single season?

   A) 4
   B) 6
   C) 8
   D) None of the above

48) How many times have Patriots head coaches been named Associated Press NFL Coach of the Year?

   A) 1
   B) 2
   C) 4
   D) 6

New England Patriots Football

Second Quarter — 2-Point Questions
Patriotology Trivia Challenge

49) How many decades have the Patriots won at least 85 games?

  A) 0
  B) 1
  C) 2
  D) 4

50) How many New England players have won Super Bowl MVP?

  A) 2
  B) 3
  C) 4
  D) 5

Second Quarter — Cool Fact
Patriotology Trivia Challenge

There have been many unlikely heroes in NFL history. No one could have ever guessed that on one snowy day at Schaefer Stadium in 1982 a prisoner on work-release would become one of them. In a game in which the Patriots and Dolphins battled the weather as much as each other, they were tied 0-0 with 4:45 left in the game. Both teams had missed two field-goal attempts earlier in the game. Enter our unlikely hero. Mark Henderson had been working all day to help clear Schaefer Stadium of the rapidly accumulating snow. He had volunteered to run the sweeper (i.e., the game should be known as the "Snow Sweeper Game") to keep the sidelines clear. It was at this moment that Patriots coach Ron Meyer took Henderson, who patiently was sitting on his John Deere tractor, up on his offer. Henderson cleared the 20-yard line swerving at just the right moment to clean the carpet at the 23-yard line where John Smith would hit the game-winning field goal. For his role in paving the way to a Patriots victory, Henderson's name would be displayed on the scoreboard to a heart-warming standing ovation from grateful Patriots fans.

Second Quarter — Answer Key
Patriotology Trivia Challenge

1) A – Patriot Place (Opened in 2008, this commercial center is home to The Hall at Patriot Place, the home of the team's hall of fame.)
2) D – No. 14 (Grogan's No. 14 has not been retired by the Patriots, but his No. 11 at Kansas State has been.)
3) A – 2006 (The Pats selected Minnesota's Laurence Maroney with the 21st overall pick of the first round in 2006.)
4) D – 2000s (Through the decade of the 2000s, the Patriots enjoyed a .700 winning percentage.)
5) A – Yes (The Patriots' all-time record versus the Colts is 45-29 [.608].)
6) B – 8 (2003 [14], 2004 [14], 2005 [10], 2006 [12], 2007 [16], 2008 [11], 2009 [10] and 2010 [14])
7) C – 112 (New England had 112 net rushing yards in Super Bowl XXXIX versus Philadelphia.)
8) A – Pacific (University of the Pacific, Stockton, California; Pete Carroll played Safety for the Tigers. Prior to transferring to the Pacific, Carroll played two seasons at the College of Marin, a junior college.)
9) D – Michigan (Ty Law played for the Wolverines from 1992-94 and Tom Brady from 1996-99.)
10) A – 4 (Buffalo [101], Indianapolis [74], Miami [91], and New York Jets [103])
11) C – 51 (On Jan. 5, 1964, the Chargers defeated the Pats 51-10 in the 1963 AFL Championship Game.)
12) B – Buffalo Bills (Patriots 28, Bills 7 at Buffalo on July 30, 1960)

New England Patriots Football

Second Quarter — Answer Key
Patriotology Trivia Challenge

13) B – No (From 2009-10, Hoyer has accumulated 42 passing attempts in the 10 games in which he has played.)
14) D – 2002 (LaDainian Tomlinson rushed for 217 yards against the Pats on Sept. 29, 2002.)
15) C – 54 yards (The 54-yard field goal was kicked by Adam Vinatieri vs. Cleveland on Dec. 12, 2001.)
16) A – 108 (It took place on Sept. 9, 2007, at the NY Jets. The 108-yard return set the NFL record for the longest-ever kickoff return and tied the record for the longest play of all time.)
17) D – 12 (This set the NFL record for this category.)
18) D – 2010 (New England had 502 total yards versus Miami [181 rushing and 321 passing] on Jan. 2, 2010.)
19) C – 5 (Jack Concannon 1964, Jim Plunkett 1971, Kenneth Sims 1982, Irving Fryar 1984 and Drew Bledsoe 1993)
20) A – True (Coach Belichick was head coach for the Cleveland Browns from 1991-95.)
21) D – 85 (New England's team record for the longest run from the line of scrimmage was set by Larry Garron versus Buffalo on Oct. 22, 1961. Garron scored a touchdown on the play.)
22) A – 5 (New England holds a 3-2 advantage in their series against the Panthers. The teams' most recent meeting was in 2009 [New England 20, Carolina 10].)

Second Quarter — Answer Key
Patriotology Trivia Challenge

23) B – 2006 (The surface was natural grass from 2002-06. It remains FieldTurf as of today.)
24) D – 7 (New England is 4-3 overall in its AFC Wild Card appearances.)
25) B – False (The Patriots have been outgained every Super Bowl in which they have played, with the exception of Super Bowl XXXVIII.)
26) D – 1963 (AFL Divisional Game at Buffalo on Dec. 28, 1963 [Patriots 26, Buffalo 8])
27) C – 12 (New England's all-time regular-season record in home openers is 16-12.)
28) A – John Smith (John Stephens received the award in 1988, Leonard Russell in 1991 and Curtis Martin in 1995.)
29) D – 16 (This is currently the Patriots' team record for most years of service by an individual player.)
30) B – 14 (The Patriots finished their first-ever season with a 5-9 overall record.)
31) D – 93 yards (On Nov. 3, 1991, Shawn McCarthy hit a 93-yard punt at Buffalo.)
32) A – True (Don Shula and George Halas are the only other NFL coaches to ever coach an undefeated regular season.)
33) C – Wes Welker (Welker set the Patriots' team record with 123 receptions in 2009.)
34) D – Terry Glenn (Glenn had 214 yards on 13 receptions at Cleveland on Oct. 3, 1999.)

Second Quarter — Answer Key
Patriotology Trivia Challenge

35) B – Dallas Texans (In the second to last game of their first season, the Patriots were shut out 0-34 at Dallas.)

36) A – Pittsburgh Steelers (The Pats defeated the Steelers 30-14 in the stadium's opening-day celebration.)

37) D – 2010 (Emphatically announcing his return following major knee surgery due to an injury in the final game of the 2009 season, Wes Welker connected with Tom Brady to cap a 72-yard season opening drive versus the Bengals.)

38) A – John Hannah (John appeared in nine Pro Bowls [1976 and 1978-85].)

39) B – Tom Brady (In 2007, Tom Brady eclipsed Drew Bledsoe's previous franchise record of 4,555 yards with 4,806 yards passing.)

40) A – True (Gostkowski set the new NFL record with 74 PATs.)

41) B – David Patten (Patten's 91-yard touchdown reception from Tom Brady at Indianapolis in 2001 is still the franchise record in this category.)

42) C – 2001 (Brady played in 15 games and started 14 of them in the 2001 season. Since then he has played in and started every regular-season game, with the exception of the 15 games started by Matt Cassel in 2008 due to Brady's injury in the season opener.)

Second Quarter — Answer Key
Patriotology Trivia Challenge

43) D – 2009 (Eric Smith of the New York Jets blocked Chris Hanson's punt resulting in a 4-yard return for a touchdown in Week 11 of the 2009 season.)

44) B – Philadelphia Eagles (Nelson holds the Patriots' team record for recovering these fumbles versus the Eagles on Oct. 8, 1978.)

45) B – No (But he was close with 29,657 total career yards from 1993-2001.)

46) D – Andre Tippett (From 1982-88 and 1990-93, Tippett recorded 100.0 career sacks for the Patriots.)

47) A – 4 (Randy Moss [1,493, 2007], Stanley Morgan [1,491, 1986], Wes Welker [1,348, 2009] and Randy Moss [1,264, 2009])

48) C – 4 (Bill Belichick in 2003, 2007 and 2010 and Bill Parcells in 1994)

49) B – 1 (The Pats recorded 112 wins in the decade of the 2000s [112-48, for a .700 winning percentage.)

50) A – 2 (Tom Brady won the award in 2002 and 2004 and Deion Branch in 2005.)

Note: All answers valid as of the end of the 2010 season, unless otherwise indicated in the question itself.

Third Quarter — 3-Point Questions
Patriotology Trivia Challenge

1) Since 1970, how many times has New England lost in the AFC Championship game?

    A) 0
    B) 1
    C) 2
    D) 3

Answers begin on page 56

2) How much did Robert Kraft pay for the Patriots in 1994?

    A) $75 million
    B) $172 million
    C) $325 million
    D) None of the above

3) Which year was New England's first-ever 10-win season?

    A) 1964
    B) 1967
    C) 1976
    D) 1978

4) Which Patriots head coach has the second most wins while at New England?

    A) Bill Parcells
    B) Raymond Berry
    C) Chuck Fairbanks
    D) Mike Holovak

Third Quarter — 3-Point Questions
Patriotology Trivia Challenge

5) What is the largest-ever margin of victory for New England in a playoff game?

   A) 15 points
   B) 20 points
   C) 25 points
   D) 30 points

6) Who holds the Patriots' career record for receiving yards?

   A) Stanley Morgan
   B) Irving Fryar
   C) Troy Brown
   D) Terry Glenn

7) Which of the following New England quarterbacks never threw five touchdown passes in a single game?

   A) Vito Parilli
   B) Steve Grogan
   C) Tom Brady
   D) Jim Plunkett

8) How many combined kickoffs and punts were returned for touchdowns by the Patriots in 2010?

   A) 0
   B) 3
   C) 5
   D) 8

New England Patriots Football

Third Quarter — 3-Point Questions
Patriotology Trivia Challenge

9) What is New England's record for PATs made in a single game?

   A) 6
   B) 7
   C) 8
   D) 9

10) What is the only decade the Patriots failed to have a 10-win season?

   A) 1960s
   B) 1970s
   C) 1980s
   D) None of the above

11) Gino Cappelletti led the league in scoring for five seasons.

   A) True
   B) False

12) In 2010, how many games did Tom Brady pass for greater than 300 yards?

   A) 0
   B) 1
   C) 3
   D) 4

Third Quarter — 3-Point Questions
Patriotology Trivia Challenge

13) How many times has a linebacker led the Patriots in sacks?

   A) 15
   B) 17
   C) 22
   D) 25

14) Who are the only Patriot defenders to record 10 interceptions in a single season?

   A) Ty Law and Ronnie Lippett
   B) Ron Hall and Asante Samuel
   C) Mike Haynes and Bob Suci
   D) Maurice Hurst and Raymond Clayborn

15) Including the postseason, which Patriots head coach has the highest all-time winning percentage?

   A) Bill Belichick
   B) Mike Holovak
   C) Chuck Fairbanks
   D) Raymond Berry

16) What is New England's record for the highest total net yards in a single game?

   A) 526
   B) 529
   C) 619
   D) 636

New England Patriots Football

Third Quarter — 3-Point Questions
Patriotology Trivia Challenge

17) What are the most yards New England has allowed in a playoff game?

   A) 610
   B) 633
   C) 698
   D) 721

18) What is the Patriots' record for the most consecutive losses?

   A) 8
   B) 10
   C) 12
   D) 14

19) When was the last time the season leading passer for New England had fewer than 1,000 yards passing?

   A) 1962
   B) 1972
   C) 1982
   D) 1992

20) Who was the most recent receiver to lead the Patriots in scoring?

   A) Ben Coates
   B) Stanley Morgan
   C) Tony Collins
   D) Randy Moss

Third Quarter — 3-Point Questions
Patriotology Trivia Challenge

21) What is the Patriots' current streak for consecutive home game sellouts?

   A) 170 games
   B) 180 games
   C) 190 games
   D) 200 games

22) The Patriots cheerleading squad was established in 1977?

   A) Yes
   B) No

23) How many seasons did Coach Belichick spend as an assistant coach for the New York Giants?

   A) 6
   B) 8
   C) 10
   D) 12

24) When was the last time the Patriots gained greater than 2,500 rushing yards as a team in a single season?

   A) 1971
   B) 1979
   C) 1983
   D) 1996

New England Patriots Football

Third Quarter — 3-Point Questions
Patriotology Trivia Challenge

25) Tom Brady has more than two times as many career pass attempts in the playoffs as Drew Bledsoe.

   A) True
   B) False

26) Against which team did New England go into overtime in 2010?

   A) Buffalo Bills
   B) Baltimore Ravens
   C) Minnesota Vikings
   D) Green Bay Packers

27) Who is the last New England player to be named UPI AFC Rookie of the Year?

   A) Mike Haynes
   B) John Stephens
   C) Curtis Martin
   D) Terry Glenn

28) Since 1970, how many times has a non-kicker led the Patriots in scoring?

   A) 4
   B) 7
   C) 9
   D) 12

Third Quarter — 3-Point Questions
Patriotology Trivia Challenge

29) Who is credited with calling the fake punt during the second quarter of the 2010 AFC Divisional game versus the New York Jets?

   A) Bill Belichick
   B) Matt Katula
   C) Patrick Chung
   D) Zoltan Mesko

30) What is the combined winning percentage for coaches who lasted only one season at New England?

   A) .091
   B) .101
   C) .191
   D) .251

31) Who was the Patriots team leader in interceptions in 2010?

   A) James Sanders
   B) Devin McCourty
   C) Brandon Meriweather
   D) Patrick Chung

32) How many teams have more all-time Super Bowl berths than the New England Patriots?

   A) 0
   B) 1
   C) 2
   D) 3

New England Patriots Football

Third Quarter — 3-Point Questions
Patriotology Trivia Challenge

33) Against which AFC teams does New England have the highest all-time winning percentage (min. 3 games)?

   A) Indianapolis Colts and Cincinnati Bengals
   B) Baltimore Ravens and Jacksonville Jaguars
   C) Tennessee Titans and Buffalo Bills
   D) San Diego Chargers and Cleveland Browns

34) How did New England score its first points in its first-ever Super Bowl?

   A) Field goal
   B) Rushing touchdown
   C) Safety
   D) Passing touchdown

35) Has New England ever failed to rush for 1,000 yards as a team in a season?

   A) Yes
   B) No

36) Who started 147 games in his career as a Patriot?

   A) Ray Hamilton
   B) Steve Grogan
   C) Raymond Clayborn
   D) Bruce Armstrong

Third Quarter — 3-Point Questions
Patriotology Trivia Challenge

37) Who was the first round pick for the Patriots in the 2011 NFL Draft?

   A) Shane Vereen
   B) Ras-I Dowling
   C) Stevan Ridley
   D) Nate Solder

38) Who is the only Patriot to lead the NFL in scoring in two consecutive seasons?

   A) John Smith
   B) Gino Cappelletti
   C) Adam Vinatieri
   D) Tony Franklin

39) Who was the holder for John Smith's infamous snowplow field goal versus Miami in 1982?

   A) Steve Grogan
   B) Tom Flick
   C) Matt Cavanaugh
   D) Don Hasselbeck

40) When was the last time the leading rusher for New England gained fewer than 500 yards for the season?

   A) 1992
   B) 1994
   C) 1996
   D) 1998

Third Quarter — 3-Point Questions
Patriotology Trivia Challenge

41) When was the last time the Patriots were undefeated in the preseason?

   A) 2001
   B) 2003
   C) 2006
   D) 2007

42) What is New England's record for the largest-ever margin of victory?

   A) 35 points
   B) 38 points
   C) 49 points
   D) 59 points

43) How many Patriots were selected to the Pro Bowl in 2010?

   A) 6
   B) 7
   C) 9
   D) 10

44) Who coached New England immediately after Mike Holovak?

   A) John Mazur
   B) Clive Rush
   C) Ron Erhardt
   D) Ron Meyer

Third Quarter — 3-Point Questions
Patriotology Trivia Challenge

45) Who scored the first touchdown for the Patriots in the 2007 AFC Championship Game versus the Chargers?

   A) Jabar Gaffney
   B) Wes Welker
   C) Laurence Maroney
   D) Randy Moss

46) Did Raymond Berry lose his last game as a Patriot head coach?

   A) Yes
   B) No

47) Where did the Patriots play their home games just prior to the opening of Foxboro Stadium in 1971?

   A) Nickerson Field
   B) Fenway Park
   C) Alumni Stadium
   D) Harvard Stadium

48) How many New England receivers had over 50 catches in the 2010 regular season?

   A) 1
   B) 2
   C) 3
   D) 4

New England Patriots Football

Third Quarter — 3-Point Questions
Patriotology Trivia Challenge

49) When was the last time New England led the NFL in rushing defense?

   A) 1965
   B) 1970
   C) 1974
   D) 1982

50) What is New England's record for the most consecutive playoff wins?

   A) 10
   B) 11
   C) 12
   D) 13

Third Quarter — Cool Fact
Patriotology Trivia Challenge

As an NFL player Raymond Berry would become the symbol of determination, hard work and perseverance. The fact that he wore special shoes to make up for varied leg length, was only of average speed and quickness, and had generally poor eyesight only made his achievements even more extraordinary. As a coach for the Patriots from 1984-89, he would use the same heart to lead the Patriots to the Super Bowl in 1985. The fascinating part of the story is not that Coach Berry turned around a struggling team, but just as in his own life, he did it against the odds. In 1985, the Patriots' road to the Super Bowl took them through New York, Los Angeles and Miami. To get to New Orleans, Coach Berry's Patriots would have to become the first team to ever win three playoff games on the road. And in true Berry form, he did just that. His teams marshaled all of their resources to win stunning victories of 26-14, 27-7 and 31-14 versus the Jets, Raiders and Dolphins respectively. His Patriots won their shot in Super Bowl XX the old-fashioned way. They earned it. Their legendary victory was just the way player Raymond Berry would have done it himself.

New England Patriots Football

Third Quarter — Answer Key
Patriotology Trivia Challenge

1) B – 1 (The Pats have a 6-1 all-time record in AFC Championship games. Their only loss was 34-38 at Indianapolis on Jan. 21, 2007.)
2) B – $172 million (Robert Kraft purchased the team from James Orthwein.)
3) A – 1964 (Although the Pats had two near misses with 9-4 records in 1961 and 1962, their first-ever 10-win season was in 1964 when they went 10-3.)
4) D – Mike Holovak (Coach Holovak had an overall record of 52-46-9 [.528] while at New England.)
5) C – 25 points (New England defeated Pittsburgh 28-3 in the 1996 AFC Divisional game and Jacksonville by the same score in the 2005 AFC Wild Card game.)
6) A – Stanley Morgan (From 1977-89, Stanley racked up 10,352 career receiving yards.)
7) D – Jim Plunkett (Many Patriots quarterbacks have thrown four touchdowns in a game, but only Tom Brady, Steve Grogan and Vito Parilli have thrown five or more.)
8) B – 3 (Julian Edelman returned one punt and Brandon Tate returned two kicks for touchdowns in 2010.)
9) C – 8 (Stephen Gostkowski made eight PATs in two games, once versus Tennessee on Oct. 18, 2009 and once at Buffalo on Nov. 18, 2007. John Smith also hit eight in a game versus the New York Jets on Sept. 9, 1979.)

New England Patriots Football

Third Quarter — Answer Key
Patriotology Trivia Challenge

10) D – None of the above (The fewest number of 10-win seasons the Pats have ever had in a decade was one. This happened in the 1960s.)
11) A – True (Cappelletti led the league in 1961 and then again from 1963-66.)
12) D – 4 (Brady had 350 yards passing at Pittsburgh, 338 yards at Detroit, 304 yards versus the New York Jets and 351 yards Chicago in 2010.)
13) C – 22 (The first was Jack Rudolph with 3.0 in the Patriots' first season [1960] and the most recent was Tully Banta-Cain with 10.0 in 2009.)
14) B – Ron Hall and Asante Samuel (Hall had 11 in 1964 and Samuel had 10 in 2006.)
15) A – Bill Belichick (Coach Belichick's overall record with the Patriots is 140-55 [.718].)
16) C – 619 (The Pats accomplished this team record versus Tennessee on Oct. 18, 2009.)
17) A – 610 (In San Diego on Jan. 5, 1964, in the 1963 AFL Championship game San Diego had 610 yards.)
18) D – 14 (The Pats lost 14 in a row from Sept. 23, 1990 to Sept. 1, 1991.)
19) C – 1982 (This has only happened one time and it was in 1982. Steve Grogan had 930 passing yards that year.)
20) D – Randy Moss (Moss led all Patriots with 138 points in 2007.)

Third Quarter
Answer Key
Patriotology Trivia Challenge

21) B – 180 (This current streak dates back to the home opener of the 1994 regular season, Robert Kraft's first season as owner of the franchise.)
22) A – Yes (Their activities include public appearances, community involvement as well as organizing the junior cheerleader squad.)
23) D – 12 (Belichick served in various assistant coaching and coordinator roles in New York from 1979-90.)
24) C – 1983 (The Pats had a team total of 2,605 yards rushing in 1983. This is only one of three seasons in which they have exceeded 2,500 yards rushing as a team. In 1978, they had 3,165 yards rushing and in 1976, they had 2,948 yards.)
25) A – True (Bledsoe had a career total 252 playoff passing attempts to Brady's 637.)
26) B – Baltimore Ravens (On Oct. 17, 2010, the Patriots and Ravens played into overtime. The Patriots went on to win the game 23-20.)
27) D – Terry Glenn (Glenn received the award in the last year it was awarded, 1996.)
28) B – 7 (Six running backs have led the team in scoring [1970, 1972, 1978, 1983, 1988 and 2010]. One wide receiver has led the team in scoring [2007].)
29) C – Patrick Chung (Chung allegedly made the call on the field due to an imbalance on the right side of the field. Chung dropped the ball on the snap leading to a busted play.)

New England Patriots Football

Third Quarter — Answer Key
Patriotology Trivia Challenge

30) A – .091 (Head coaches Bengtson, Bullough and Rust were 2-20 combined.)
31) B – Devin McCourty (McCourty accounted for a team-leading seven interceptions in 2010.)
32) C – 2 (The Cowboys and Steelers are the only two teams in the NFL with more Super Bowl Berths than the Patriots [Dallas and Pittsburgh each have eight and New England has six].)
33) B – Baltimore Ravens and Jacksonville Jaguars (All time, the Patriots are 6-1 versus Baltimore and 8-1 versus the Jaguars, for a combined winning percentage of .875.)
34) A – Field goal (Tony Franklin hit a 36-yard field goal in the first quarter of the game.)
35) B – No (In 1970, the Patriots narrowly missed going below the 1,000-yard mark as a team. They could only manage 1,040 team rushing yards that year.)
36) C – Raymond Clayborn (Clayborn was a Patriots starter from Sept. 3, 1978 to Nov. 22, 1987.)
37) D – Nate Solder (New England selected Solder with the 17th overall pick in the first round of the 2011 draft.)
38) A – John Smith (He did it in 1979 and 1980.)
39) C – Matt Cavanaugh (Quarterback Matt Cavanaugh put down the hold on the freshly swept 23-yard line for John Smi th's game-winning field goal.)
40) A – 1992 (Leading rusher Jon Vaughn had 451 yards on 113 attempts, for a 4.0 per carry average.)

New England Patriots Football

Third Quarter
Answer Key
Patriotology Trivia Challenge

41) B – 2003 (New England defeated the New York Giants [26-6], Washington [20-13], Philadelphia [24-12] and Chicago [38-23].)
42) D – 59 points (On Oct. 18, 2009, New England defeated Tennessee 59-0 to set a new team record in the category.)
43) A – 6 (Tom Brady, Wes Welker, Randy Moss, Logan Mankins, Vince Wilfork and Brandon Meriweather)
44) B – Clive Rush (Coach Rush took over head coaching duties from Coach Holovak in 1969.)
45) C – Laurence Maroney (A 1-yard touchdown run at 13:48 of the second quarter)
46) A – Yes (On Dec. 24, 1989, the Pats fell to the L.A. Rams 20-24 at home in Coach Berry's final game as head coach.)
47) D – Harvard Stadium (In preparation for the completion of Foxboro Stadium, New England played its 1970 home games at Harvard Stadium.)
48) A – 1 (Wes Welker had 86 receptions for 848 yards.)
49) C – 1974 (The Patriots' defense allowed a league-leading 1,587 yards [113.4 yards per game].)
50) A – 10 (It extends from the 2001 AFC Divisional game versus Oakland through the 2005 AFC Wild Card game versus Jacksonville.)

Note: All answers valid as of the end of the 2010 season, unless otherwise indicated in the question itself.

Fourth Quarter — 4-Point Questions
Patriotology Trivia Challenge

1) When was the last time a Patriots' game resulted in a tie?

   A) 1967
   B) 1971
   C) 1973
   D) 1977

Answers begin on page 75

2) Which opponent handed New England its worst defeat in 2010?

   A) New York Jets
   B) Green Bay Packers
   C) Pittsburgh Steelers
   D) Cleveland Browns

3) How many Patriots players have had their jersey number retired?

   A) 6
   B) 7
   C) 8
   D) 9

4) Has a Patriots running back ever had five rushing touchdowns in a single game?

   A) Yes
   B) No

New England Patriots Football

Fourth Quarter — 4-Point Questions
Patriotology Trivia Challenge

5) Which Patriot kicked the most field goals with no misses in a single game?

   A) Jason Staurovsky
   B) Adam Vinatieri
   C) Gino Cappelletti
   D) Matt Bahr

6) Who was the most recent Patriots head coach to win his first-ever regular-season game?

   A) Dick MacPherson
   B) Bill Belichick
   C) Bill Parcells
   D) Pete Carroll

7) The Patriots are 11-3 all time in playoff games at home.

   A) True
   B) False

8) How many Patriots head coaches are in the Pro Football Hall of Fame?

   A) 0
   B) 1
   C) 2
   D) 3

Fourth Quarter / 4-Point Questions
Patriotology Trivia Challenge

9) Against which AFC team does New England have the lowest all-time winning percentage (min. 3 games)?

   A) Kansas City Chiefs
   B) Tennessee Titans
   C) Pittsburgh Steelers
   D) Denver Broncos

10) Did Bill Belichick have a winning record when coaching against the Patriots?

    A) Yes
    B) No

11) Which of the following Patriots was not named an AP All-Pro in 2010?

    A) Jerod Mayo
    B) Logan Mankins
    C) Devin McCourty
    D) Tom Brady

12) When was the last time the Patriots had two players gain over 100 yards rushing in the same game?

    A) 1979
    B) 1980
    C) 1981
    D) 1982

New England Patriots Football

Fourth Quarter — 4-Point Questions
Patriotology Trivia Challenge

13) In which of the following categories did Randy Moss lead the NFL in 2007?

   A) Touchdown Receptions
   B) Receiving Yards
   C) Yards per Reception
   D) Yards per Game

14) Who is the only Patriot to score two safeties in a single season?

   A) Ty Warren
   B) Don Blackmon
   C) Raymond Clayborn
   D) Mike Haynes

15) When was the last time the Patriots scored a touchdown on offense, defense and special teams in the same game?

   A) 2001
   B) 2002
   C) 2004
   D) 2010

16) Excluding 2008, Tom Brady has passed for greater than 3,000 yards each of his seasons with New England.

   A) True
   B) False

Fourth Quarter 4-Point Questions
Patriotology Trivia Challenge

17) How many seasons has assistant coach Pepper Johnson been with the Patriots?

   A) 11
   B) 12
   C) 13
   D) 14

18) When was the last time the Patriots had two receivers with over 1,000 yards receiving in the same season?

   A) 1981
   B) 2000
   C) 2007
   D) 2010

19) Who holds New England's record for rushing touchdowns in a career?

   A) Corey Dillon
   B) Jim Nance
   C) Sam Cunningham
   D) Curtis Martin

20) Which New England quarterback holds the game, season and career records for highest completion percentage?

   A) Steve Grogan
   B) Babe Parilli
   C) Tony Eason
   D) Tom Brady

New England Patriots Football

Fourth Quarter — 4-Point Questions
Patriotology Trivia Challenge

21) All time, how many head coaches have the Patriots had in their history?

   A) 15
   B) 17
   C) 19
   D) 21

22) What is New England's largest margin of victory over the Colts?

   A) 21 points
   B) 28 points
   C) 32 points
   D) 39 points

23) Which head coach has the second highest career winning percentage at New England (min. 3 seasons)?

   A) Mike Holovak
   B) Chuck Fairbanks
   C) Raymond Berry
   D) Pete Carroll

24) Has New England played every NFL team at least once?

   A) Yes
   B) No

Fourth Quarter — 4-Point Questions
Patriotology Trivia Challenge

25) Which Patriot player won the Ed Block Courage Award in 2010?

    A) Danny Woodhead
    B) Alge Crumpler
    C) Stephen Gostkowski
    D) Wes Welker

26) New England has an all-time winning record against every AFC East opponent.

    A) True
    B) False

27) With three Super Bowl victories by the Patriots from 2001-04, Foxborough, Mass. is now often referred to as the new what?

    A) Super City
    B) Victory Village
    C) Titletown
    D) Winners Circle

28) Who is the Patriots' all-time career leader in kickoff returns yardage?

    A) David Meggett
    B) Troy Brown
    C) Larry Garron
    D) Kevin Faulk

New England Patriots Football 67

Fourth Quarter — 4-Point Questions
Patriotology Trivia Challenge

29) In which decade did New England have its lowest-ever winning percentage?

   A) 1960s
   B) 1980s
   C) 1990s
   D) 2000s

30) The Patriots' offense was penalized for over 1,000 yards in 2010.

   A) True
   B) False

31) When was the last time the Patriots rushed for over 300 yards as a team in a single game?

   A) 1983
   B) 1989
   C) 1994
   D) 1998

32) How many combined points did the Patriots and Giants score in the 3rd quarter of Super Bowl XLII?

   A) 3
   B) 7
   C) 10
   D) None of the above

Fourth Quarter — 4-Point Questions
Patriotology Trivia Challenge

33) When was the last time the Patriots gave up a safety?

   A) 2004
   B) 2005
   C) 2006
   D) 2007

34) What is the largest margin of defeat New England has suffered in a playoff game?

   A) 40 points
   B) 41 points
   C) 42 points
   D) 43 points

35) What is New England's record for the most consecutive regular-season wins?

   A) 16
   B) 18
   C) 21
   D) 25

36) Randy Moss was named AFC Offensive Player of the Week twice in 2007?

   A) Yes
   B) No

Fourth Quarter — 4-Point Questions
Patriotology Trivia Challenge

37) How many stripes are on the sleeves of a Patriots home and away jerseys?

   A) 1
   B) 2
   C) 3
   D) 4

38) Who was the most recent Patriot to have multiple blocked kicks in a game?

   A) Kelley Washington
   B) Troy Brown
   C) Chad Eaton
   D) Richard Seymour

39) Who holds New England's record for the most consecutive seasons leading the team in sacks?

   A) Andre Tippett
   B) Rosevelt Colvin
   C) Larry Eisenhauer
   D) Tony McGee

40) In 2007, Patriot Junior Seau became the oldest player to make two or more interceptions in an NFL game?

   A) Yes
   B) No

Fourth Quarter — 4-Point Questions
Patriotology Trivia Challenge

41) How big is the largest official crowd to ever watch a Patriots' football game at home?

    A) 65,674
    B) 66,833
    C) 67,921
    D) 68,756

42) How many playoff wins did New England have in the decade of the 2000s?

    A) 12
    B) 13
    C) 14
    D) 15

43) Which of the following Patriots quarterbacks never had a 400-yard passing game?

    A) Hugh Millen
    B) Drew Bledsoe
    C) Steve Grogan
    D) Tom Ramsey

44) What was the highest winning percentage of a New England head coach who lasted only one season?

    A) .000
    B) .063
    C) .181
    D) .200

New England Patriots Football

Fourth Quarter — 4-Point Questions
Patriotology Trivia Challenge

45) Who was the most recent opponent New England shut out?

    A) Buffalo Bills
    B) Tennessee Titans
    C) Carolina Panthers
    D) Denver Broncos

46) Who holds New England's record for the most points scored in a single season?

    A) Gino Cappelletti
    B) Randy Moss
    C) Tony Franklin
    D) Adam Vinatieri

47) What is the Patriots' all-time record in snow games played in Foxborough?

    A) 7-2
    B) 8-1
    C) 11-0
    D) Stat is not kept

48) What is New England's record for the most consecutive wins at home?

    A) 15
    B) 16
    C) 17
    D) 18

Fourth Quarter — 4-Point Questions
Patriotology Trivia Challenge

49) Who holds New England's career rushing record in the playoffs?

   A) Kevin Faulk
   B) Craig James
   C) Corey Dillon
   D) Tony Collins

50) What is written directly underneath the giant "Gillette Stadium" sign near the main entrance to the stadium?

   A) Home of the New England Patriots
   B) Three-Time World Champions
   C) Home of the Super Bowl Champions
   D) Home of the NFL's Greatest Fans

Fourth Quarter

Patriotology Trivia Challenge

Cool Fact

Robert Kraft to the rescue! In 1994 New England was on the verge of suffering the same fate its arch rival Baltimore had endured exactly one decade earlier. Then Patriots owner James Orthwein, a wealthy St. Louis, Missouri businessman, was posturing to move the team to his hometown – robbing New England of its beloved Patriots. Although Orthwein did not necessarily intend to move the team under the cover of darkness, like Colts owner Bob Irsay had done, nonetheless such an act would have robbed a city of a team they had grown to love and cherish. It was at that moment that Robert Kraft chose to forego a $75 million buyout of the Patriots' lease on Foxboro Stadium for a much riskier investment of $172 million into the Patriots franchise. In addition, Kraft Group would go on to invest $325 million in the development of Patriot Place. Kraft's commitment to the Patriots and to New England in general continues to pay big dividends. It resulted in the hiring of Coach Belichick and helped pave the way for the team's and region's many successes since that fateful 1994 decision.

Fourth Quarter — Answer Key
Patriotology Trivia Challenge

1) A – 1967 (On Oct. 8, 1967, the Patriots and the Chargers played to a 31-31 tie in San Diego.)
2) D – Cleveland Browns (The Browns handed the Pats a 14-34 loss in Week 9. The 20-point loss was New England's largest margin of defeat for the season.)
3) C – 8 (Gino Cappelletti [No. 20], Mike Haynes [No. 40], Andre Tippett [No. 56], Steve Nelson [No. 57], John Hannah [No. 73], Bruce Armstrong [No. 78], Jim Hunt [No. 79] and Bob Dee [No. 89])
4) B – No (Several Patriots running backs have scored three rushing touchdowns in a game, but no one has ever scored more than three in a single game.)
5) C – Gino Cappelletti (Gino was six for six versus Denver on Oct. 4, 1964 [New England 39, Denver 10].)
6) D – Pete Carroll (Carroll's debut as Patriots head coach in 1997 resulted in a 41-7 victory over San Diego.)
7) A – True (The most recent home playoff game was played on Jan. 16, 2011. The Jets stunned the Pats with a 28-21 victory in the AFC Divisional game.)
8) A – 0 (To date no Patriots coaches have been inducted into the Pro Football Hall of Fame.)
9) D – Denver Broncos (The Pats have an all-time record of 16-27 versus the Broncos [.372].)
10) A – Yes (From 1991-95, as head coach of the Browns, Coach Belichick had a 4-2 record versus the Pats.)
11) C – Devin McCourty (McCourty was named an All-Pro by *The Sporting News*, not the AP. All others listed received AP First Team honors in 2010.)

New England Patriots Football

Fourth Quarter — Answer Key
Patriotology Trivia Challenge

12) D – 1982 (Tony Collins had 103 yards rushing and Mark van Eeghen had exactly 100 at Seattle on Dec. 19, 1982.)

13) A – Touchdown Receptions (Moss eclipsed Jerry Rice's previous record of 22 touchdown receptions in a season with 23.)

14) B – Don Blackmon (In 1985, Blackmon scored one safety versus Green Bay and one at Tampa Bay.)

15) D – 2010 (The Pats last accomplished this feat on Oct. 4, 2010, at Miami [New England 41, Miami 14].)

16) B – False (In 2000, Brady played in one game passing for 6 yards. In 2001, he nearly reached the 3,000-yard milestone with 2,843 yards on the season. From 2002-present he has surpassed the 3,000-yard mark each year, with the exception of the injury season of 2008.)

17) A – 11 (The 2011 season will mark Johnson's 12th season as an assistant coach to Bill Belichick.)

18) C – 2007 (In 2007 Randy Moss had 1,493 receiving yards and Wes Welker had 1,175.)

19) B – Jim Nance (From 1965-71 Nance scored 45 rushing touchdowns for the Patriots.)

20) D – Tom Brady (Brady's team records for completion percentage are .636 for his career [2000-10], .689 for a season [2007] and .885 for a game [vs. Jacksonville on Dec. 27, 2009].)

21) A – 15 (Bill Belichick is New England's 15th head coach of all time.)

Fourth Quarter — Answer Key
Patriotology Trivia Challenge

22) D – 39 points (On Oct. 6, 1974, the Patriots convincingly defeated the Colts 42-3 at home.)
23) C – Raymond Berry (Berry had a career record of 51-41 from 1984-89, a .554 winning percentage.)
24) A – Yes (This ranges from 104 all-time games versus the New York Jets to three games versus the Houston Texans.)
25) D – Wes Welker (The award is given annually by each team to a player who "best exemplifies the principles of courage and sportsmanship while also serving as a source of inspiration.")
26) B – False (New England's all-time record versus Buffalo is 61-40-1, versus Miami it is 41-50 and versus the New York Jets it is 51-52-1.)
27) C – Titletown (This is a popular nickname given to a multi-year championship team's hometown by their fans, the press and others.)
28) D – Kevin Faulk (From 1999-2010, Faulk amassed 4,098 total return yards. The next nearest player is Ellis Hobbs with 2,913 from 2005-08.)
29) C – 1990s (The Pats had a historic low .425 winning percentage in the 1990s [68-92 record].)
30) B – False (The Pats' offense was penalized 83 times for 766 yards in the 2010 regular season.)
31) A – 1983 (On Sept. 18, 1983, the Patriots rushed for a team total 328 net yards vs. the New York Jets.)

Fourth Quarter — Answer Key
Patriotology Trivia Challenge

32) D – None of the above (Neither the Patriots nor the Giants scored any points in the 3rd quarter of Super Bowl XLII.)

33) C – 2006 (On Dec. 3, 2006, Quarterback Tom Brady was sacked and the ball was recovered in the end zone by the Detroit Lions' Heath Evans.)

34) B – 41 points (San Diego defeated New England 51-10 at home in the 1963 AFL Championship game on Jan. 1, 1964.)

35) C – 21 (From the Dec. 17, 2006, 40-7 win versus Houston to the Sept. 14, 2008, 19-10 win at the New York Jets the Patriots won 21 consecutive regular-season games.)

36) A – Yes (Moss was AFC Offensive Player of the Week for Weeks 9 and 11.)

37) A – 1 (Current jerseys have one large asymmetrical strip just at the edge of the shoulder pads. Alternate jerseys have three stripes across the shoulder pads.)

38) C – Chad Eaton (On Dec. 17, 2000, Eaton blocked two field goal attempts at Buffalo.)

39) D – Tony McGee (McGee led the team in sacks from 1975-79. He is the only player to lead the team in sacks for five consecutive years.)

40) A – Yes (Seau had two interceptions versus Cleveland on Oct. 7, 2007, to set this NFL record.)

41) D – 68,756 (This matches the official seating capacity of Gillette Stadium.)

Fourth Quarter — Answer Key
Patriotology Trivia Challenge

42) C – 14 (This ties the NFL record which is co-held with the Cowboys and the Steelers of the 1970s.)

43) A – Hugh Millen (Drew Bledsoe had 426 yards versus Minnesota, Steve Grogan had 401 yards versus the New York Jets and Tom Ramsey had 402 yards versus Philadelphia. Millen is not noted as having ever passed for greater than 400 yards.)

44) D – .200 (One-season Patriots head coach Phil Bengtson was 1-4 in 1972.)

45) B – Tennessee Titans (The Pats handed the Titans a 59-0 loss in Week 6 of the 2009 season.)

46) A – Gino Cappelletti (Cappelletti had 7 TDs, 36 PATs and 25 FGs for 155 total points in the 1964 season.)

47) C – 11-0 (Since 1971, the Patriots have an enviable record of 11-0 in games in which snow has fallen during the game in Foxborough.)

48) D – 18 (The Pats won 18 straight at home from Dec. 29, 2002 to Sept. 8, 2005.)

49) C – Corey Dillon (In eight playoff games as a Patriot, Dillon rushed for a team playoff record 508 total yards.)

50) A – Home of the New England Patriots (It is written in all-caps in white lettering.)

Note: All answers valid as of the end of the 2010 season, unless otherwise indicated in the question itself.

Overtime Bonus — 4-Point Questions
Patriotology Trivia Challenge

1) Which Patriot caught the most touchdown passes in a career?

   A) Ben Coates
   B) Gino Cappelletti
   C) Troy Brown
   D) Stanley Morgan

Answers begin on page 83

2) What is the longest winning streak for the Patriots in the New England-Colts series?

   A) 5 games
   B) 6 games
   C) 7 games
   D) 8 games

3) How many Pro Bowl appearances has Tom Brady had in his career in New England?

   A) 6
   B) 7
   C) 8
   D) 9

4) New England has the highest playoff winning percentage in the NFL (minimum 20 postseason games).

   A) True
   B) False

New England Patriots Football

Overtime Bonus / 4-Point Questions
Patriotology Trivia Challenge

5) Who was the most recent quarterback to throw five TD passes against the Patriots?

    A) Eli Manning
    B) Dan Marino
    C) Kurt Warner
    D) A.J. Freeley

6) Other than Coach Belichick, how many NFL head coaches have won 100 or more games with their current team?

    A) 1
    B) 2
    C) 3
    D) 5

7) What year did the Patriots finish the season with only one win?

    A) 1988
    B) 1989
    C) 1990
    D) 1991

8) Who is the only Patriot to be named Pro Bowl MVP?

    A) Ty Law
    B) Tom Brady
    C) Ben Coates
    D) Marv Cook

New England Patriots Football

Overtime Bonus — 4-Point Questions
Patriotology Trivia Challenge

9) Who holds the Patriots' record for the most games played in a career?

    A) Mosi Tatupu
    B) Troy Brown
    C) Julius Adams
    D) Bruce Armstrong

10) What are the most points ever scored by New England in a single game?

    A) 53
    B) 59
    C) 63
    D) 66

Overtime Bonus — Answer Key
Patriotology Trivia Challenge

1) D – Stanley Morgan (WR, 67 TD receptions)
2) C – 7 games (This lasted from their first matchup of 1996 to first matchup of 1999.)
3) A – 6 (Brady appeared in the 2001, 2004, 2005, 2007, 2009 and 2010 Pro Bowls.)
4) B – False (The Pittsburgh Steelers, Green Bay Packers and San Francisco 49ers all have higher postseason winning percentages.)
5) B – Dan Marino (Sept. 4, 1996 at Miami)
6) A – 1 (Philadelphia's Andy Reid has 118 career wins for the Eagles.)
7) C – 1990 (1-15 in Coach Rust's only season)
8) A – Ty Law (Co-MVP with Keyshawn Johnson, 1998)
9) D – Bruce Armstrong (Armstrong played in 212 games from 1987-2000.)
10) B – 59 (On Oct. 18, 2009, the Pats scored 59 points versus the Tennessee Titans [New England 59, Tennessee 0].)

Note: All answers valid as of the end of the 2010 season, unless otherwise indicated in the question itself.

New England Patriots Football

Player / Team Score Sheet

Name:_____

First Quarter		Second Quarter		Third Quarter		Fourth Quarter		Overtime Bonus	
1	26	1	26	1	26	1	26	1	
2	27	2	27	2	27	2	27	2	
3	28	3	28	3	28	3	28	3	
4	29	4	29	4	29	4	29	4	
5	30	5	30	5	30	5	30	5	
6	31	6	31	6	31	6	31	6	
7	32	7	32	7	32	7	32	7	
8	33	8	33	8	33	8	33	8	
9	34	9	34	9	34	9	34	9	
10	35	10	35	10	35	10	35	10	
11	36	11	36	11	36	11	36		
12	37	12	37	12	37	12	37		
13	38	13	38	13	38	13	38		
14	39	14	39	14	39	14	39		
15	40	15	40	15	40	15	40		
16	41	16	41	16	41	16	41		
17	42	17	42	17	42	17	42		
18	43	18	43	18	43	18	43		
19	44	19	44	19	44	19	44		
20	45	20	45	20	45	20	45		
21	46	21	46	21	46	21	46		
22	47	22	47	22	47	22	47		
23	48	23	48	23	48	23	48		
24	49	24	49	24	49	24	49		
25	50	25	50	25	50	25	50		
___ x 1 = ___		___ x 2 = ___		___ x 3 = ___		___ x 4 = ___		___ x 4 = ___	

Multiply total number correct by point value/quarter to calculate totals for each quarter.

Add total of all quarters below.

Total Points:_____

Thank you for playing *Patriotology Trivia Challenge*.

Additional score sheets are available at:
www.TriviaGameBooks.com

Player / Team Score Sheet

Name:_____

First Quarter	Second Quarter	Third Quarter	Fourth Quarter	Overtime Bonus
1	1	1	1	1
2	2	2	2	2
3	3	3	3	3
4	4	4	4	4
5	5	5	5	5
6	6	6	6	6
7	7	7	7	7
8	8	8	8	8
9	9	9	9	9
10	10	10	10	10
11	11	11	11	
12	12	12	12	
13	13	13	13	
14	14	14	14	
15	15	15	15	
16	16	16	16	
17	17	17	17	
18	18	18	18	
19	19	19	19	
20	20	20	20	
21	21	21	21	
22	22	22	22	
23	23	23	23	
24	24	24	24	
25	25	25	25	
26	26	26	26	
27	27	27	27	
28	28	28	28	
29	29	29	29	
30	30	30	30	
31	31	31	31	
32	32	32	32	
33	33	33	33	
34	34	34	34	
35	35	35	35	
36	36	36	36	
37	37	37	37	
38	38	38	38	
39	39	39	39	
40	40	40	40	
41	41	41	41	
42	42	42	42	
43	43	43	43	
44	44	44	44	
45	45	45	45	
46	46	46	46	
47	47	47	47	
48	48	48	48	
49	49	49	49	
50	50	50	50	
___ x 1 = ___	___ x 2 = ___	___ x 3 = ___	___ x 4 = ___	___ x 4 = ___

Multiply total number correct by point value/quarter to calculate totals for each quarter.

Add total of all quarters below.

Total Points:_____

Thank you for playing ***Patriotology Trivia Challenge***.

**Additional score sheets are available at:
www.TriviaGameBooks.com**